Funeral
Source
Book

Funeral Source Book

Thoughts for Funerals and Other Occasions

R. Earl Allen

PULPIT LIBRARY

BAKER BOOK HOUSE Grand Rapids, Michigan 49506

Copyright 1964 by Broadman Press
Formerly published under the title:
Memorial Messages

Paperback edition issued 1974 by
Baker Book House
with the permission of the
copyright holder

ISBN: 0-8010-0076-9

Seventh printing, June 1989

Dewey Decimal Classification: 252
Library of Congress Catalog Card Number 64-12408
Printed in the United States of America

Foreword

It is a distinct privilege to write a brief foreword to this book. I have known the author for almost two decades. Every Sunday he preaches to more people in a single service than nine out of ten of our Southern Baptist pastors. He is a lover of men's souls. He knows more people, talks to more people, wins more people to Christ than almost any pastor I know. His soul was touched to tenderness and understanding by a great sorrow which might have wrecked lesser men. It was my honor to be among those who shared his agony. In that hour my soul received fresh spiritual impetus and vision as I watched him practice the truths set forth in this book. He would be the last to suspect that God has given him a special ministry of comfort to the sorrowing. Truths which are self-evident to him heal like a balm when applied to aching hearts. I shared the conviction, held by many of his friends, that he should commit these memorial messages to print. I am personally delighted that he has finally consented to do so.

Two classes of readers will take up this volume of

memorial messages. The one class will find in it things which satisfy and help the soul when buffeted with adverse winds and tides. Its truths will stand out to them like flashes struck from midnight. The other class will read, mark, learn, and inwardly digest its contents in order to comfort others with the comfort set forth herein. Thus all will be blessed.

CARL E. BATES

Pastor's Study
First Baptist Church
Charlotte, North Carolina

Preface

Memorial messages, of all sermons, are the most difficult to commit to the printed page. A funeral service is always designed to meet personal need rather than for popular appeal. The manner and method of the minister, as well as his message, determine the mood of the memorial service. These intangibles are hard to reproduce in print.

Never will the minister speak to a more captive audience. It is also the time when he speaks to those other than members of his own congregation. On such occasions, the people gather in a common bond of love and sympathy. The minister speaks truly as "God's man." The people wish to hear God's message for such a time.

The customs of the memorial service vary from community to city, and from church to minister. The wishes of the family are primary. Also, the practices of the funeral establishment must be considered. Music is a vital means of communication in Christianity, and the selections should be such as would reaffirm our faith.

Any minister feels ill-prepared to face the constant

perplexing problem of the preparation of funeral messages. His primary purpose must be to comfort hurt hearts from the Word of God. His method will vary according to his knowledge of the people and with God-given impressions.

It is my own practice to use a message on the comfort of God or the love of God at the funeral of a person who is not known to be a Christian. The loved ones must be reassured that God has not forsaken them even though he was forsaken.

When it is possible, I do not read the obituary. Rather, I fit the basic material into the message as a eulogy. From my observation, it seems that the thing that comforts the hearts of people most is a personal word concerning their loved one and a positive word from God's Book. However, it must be remembered that personal sentiments are not helpful if they are not truthful. Only a life that exalts our Lord is to be praised (Matt. 5:16; Prov. 31:31).

I am deeply grateful for the wise counsel of my preacher brethren who have shared with me their own experiences. I shall ever be in debt to the friends who have shared my life and encouraged me to write these messages. May I also express my appreciation to the members of my family who have shared my ministry and to Mrs. Alfred A. Brian, Jr. and to Miss Arline Harris for their dedication in the preparation of the manuscript.

R. EARL ALLEN

Contents

This message was prepared for a seventeen-year-old youth, Larry Bob Horn, who met with an untimely accidental death.

1

Sudden Step

1 Samuel 20:3

Amos, the ancient prophet, quoted the Lord as saying, "I will cause the sun to go down at noon" (8:9). The words of the weeping prophet, Jeremiah, more clearly describe our hearts than any words we know: "[His] sun is gone down while it was yet day" (15:9). While the sun was at its meridian, it suddenly became night for the family and friends of this youth. Job also speaks of such a one: "The number of his months is cut off in the midst. . . . One dieth in his full strength" (21:21-23).

The sadness of death seems less severe when the sun goes down in the evening. It is not so difficult to adjust our minds to the expectation of death when the three-score and ten years arrive. It is the natural thinking of parents that we shall live to see our children grown and that they will bear us to our last resting place. But, alas, in the reality of life this is not always true. Nature has its seasons. Death knows no season. It can snatch the bloom of youth as suddenly as touch the pallor of the aged.

With the realization that our young friend had heeded

11

the words of the ancient man of wisdom, "Remember now thy Creator in the days of thy youth" (Eccl. 12:1), our sorrow is lightened. We are comforted that this fine young man was contemplating the ministry and had made the Lord first in his life. He was active in all phases of our church life. He was winsome at home, at school, and at church alike. He was warm and enthusiastic and had a smile a "face wide." He was thoughtful to the old, likeable to other youth, and attentive to the very young. His work in the Chapel Choir had come to be one of the things he most enthusiastically enjoyed.

It is not necessary to prove anything to our Lord, for he knows us. It is not necessary to prove anything to our parents, for they understand us. It is not necessary to prove anything to our friends, for they love us. But often it is necessary to prove something to ourselves. This young person could live with himself, for he had proved himself a man in all realms of life. With sheer will power he set out to make the high school athletic team. With his dogged determination he won the friendship of his classmates and the respect of the coaches and teachers. We honor him today because he had prayed the prayer of the psalmist, "Teach us to number our days, that we may apply our hearts unto wisdom" (90:12).

Sadness of Shock.—David realized, at one point in his young manhood, that "there is but a step between me and death" (1 Sam. 20:3). Our minds can focus in reality upon death as a "step." The thought causes us to reflect on the brevity of life, for people of all ages fall into the hands of life's last enemy. In Proverbs 27:1, we are reminded that we know "not what a day may bring forth."

Jesus warned, "Watch ye therefore: for ye know not when the master of the house cometh" (Mark 13:35).

Surely this untimely passing is a reminder to the great host of young people gathered here of the uncertainty of life. Those who remain must surely realize that life "is even a vapour, that appeareth for a little time, and then vanisheth away" (James 4:14). The suddenness of death brings sadness and shock to our hearts, and from the depths of our souls we cannot but wonder why. There are many things that men do not understand and will not understand until we are gathered home. We do not understand the "why" that went unanswered from the lips of Jesus—himself the only begotten Son of God—as he died that we might have life.

Serenity of Security.—When such days come that try men's souls, often Christian parents are asked how they can bear up under such burdens. They can "bear up" only because they have the knowledge that their child is now with the Heavenly Father and that they, too, will one day be reunited with him. Our blessed Saviour never told a family not to weep. We remember with great comfort that "Jesus wept" (John 11:35). Paul said that we are not to mourn as those who have no hope. The great hope of the Christian is reunion with departed loved ones. David said concerning his son, "I shall go to him, but he shall not return to me" (2 Sam. 12:23).

We have the security of knowing that this body is only a temporary dwelling place. We know that instantaneously, when death comes, God's child is in the bosom of the Father. Let us not feel that it is a pity for youth to die, nor should we think for a moment that heaven is no more than a glorified old folk's home. It is the dwelling place of our Father. It is the place where the angelic choirs sing forever. It is the place of no hurt or harm; it is the place of no pain or death or sorrow.

Heaven is indescribably better than anything in this life. The apostle Paul said, "For to me to live is Christ, and to die is gain" (Phil. 1:21). Jesus said, when he went away, "I go to prepare a place for you" (John 14:2). What our blessed Lord has been preparing for these two thousand years is far more beautiful than our finite minds allow us to consider. "Eye hath not seen, nor ear heard, neither have entered into the heart of man, the things which God hath prepared for them that love him" (1 Cor. 2:9).

Shadow of Soul.—The Lord has not promised to exempt us from the shadows of sorrows. He promised that he would walk with us and never leave us alone. "Yea, though I walk through the valley of the shadow of death, I will fear no evil: for thou art with me; thy rod and thy staff they comfort me" (Psalm 23:4). There is such a thing as sweet sorrow. It is not morbid to remember the love of yesterday or the glory of youth.

When the shadows fall, we can "be still, and know that [God is] God" (Psalm 46:10). Even in this shadow we receive strength as we know that this young man was saved here, and therefore we know that he is safe there. We recognize today the sympathy of friends here and also the presence of him who is the Friend above all friends.

In these dark shadows our strength is renewed to press on by reading again the words this young man wrote to his family a brief time ago on the flyleaf of a Bible, "I never can recall a time that you have not lived up to the teachings of this book. . . . I shall always treasure it and try to keep it, until I join my Lord. You and mother have had a great and wonderful influence upon me. God bless you and be with you forever and ever." How precious and prophetic the phrase, "until I join my Lord." This indeed he has done. For the Christian there is life in the place of death, for Jesus said, "I am the resurrection, and the life: he that believeth in me, though he were dead, yet shall he live: and whosoever liveth and believeth in me shall never die" (John 11:25-26).

2

Can We Know Why?

John 13:7

Sympathy makes all men brothers. From all walks of life, as friends, we turn aside to be with this grieving family. The circumstances that bring us together find tender response in our hearts. All our hearts are heavy in the midst of sadness and sorrow that seems to have no rhyme or reason.

The psalmist cried out the question which is unspoken in so many of our hearts today, "Hath God forgotten to be gracious? hath he in anger shut up his tender mercies?" (77:9). When faith falters under circumstances that we cannot understand, we cry out with Martha, "Lord, if thou hadst been here, my brother had not died" (John 11:32). But our gracious God is here, just as he was on his throne when his own Son died.

We do not understand death, though we are vividly acquainted with its damaging power. The cry of death began with Adam and Eve when their son Abel was slain. One of the darkest nights in all history was when the firstborn in every Egyptian home died. The cry of

16

fathers and mothers and brothers and sisters has not ceased from the time of Adam until now. It will not cease until time shall be no more and Jesus shall claim final victory over that powerful "last enemy."

Even today, some eighty-six thousand of our population will meet their Maker. Some pass beyond the veil of tears without the presence of nurses, doctors, family, or friends, but it is never necessary to pass from this life without the presence of Jesus. His presence is one sure promise that every Christian has. The human question often arises, "If God be with us, then why does death come to us?" Perfect knowledge seems to be an ever-evasive truth. The Son of God asked why, just as do we on this dark day in our own hurt hearts.

Spiritual maturity comes when we recognize that there are some unknowable sorrows in life. We trust in God who is omniscient and knoweth all things. Jesus said to Simon Peter, "What I do thou knowest not now; but thou shalt know hereafter" (John 13:7). There is much that we as Christians do not know. Simon Peter did not understand the act of humility on the part of his Lord.

This would teach us that we who are finite cannot possibly understand the infinite mind of God. Our knowledge is not sufficient to grope the depths of man's problems. Why? We don't know, we don't understand. Even if we did fully understand, our hearts would still hurt. We do not think with our minds today but with our emotions, our hearts. And we cry out in pathos, "Lord, what *can* we know for sure?" The great apostle Paul knew that there would be times when our faith would falter. He understood that man's counsel would not be enough; a word from God would be needed. The divine writer was moved to say, "For this we say unto you by the word of the Lord" (1 Thess. 4:15). God has a word for every heartache. The Great Physician has a touch for every wounded spirit. The blessed Saviour has a comfort for every tear.

We do not come to this sad hour to speculate on the things that we do not understand. We come rather in our faith to grasp the certainties of life which are sure and steadfast.

We Can Remember Our Creator in Youth.—He who was given unusual human wisdom cried out, "Remember now thy Creator in the days of thy youth, while the evil days come not, nor the years draw nigh, when thou shalt say, I have no pleasure in them" (Eccl. 12:1). Death is never untimely when it is expected. When our loved ones are prepared for this sad hour, death cannot possibly slip up on us. When we have made preparations for the passage, the grave holds no final terror. The brevity of life always serves to remind us that our days on earth are few and cannot be numbered. Should we live out our three-score and ten it will seem even then as the ancient one has said, "We spend our years as a tale that is told" (Psalm 90:9).

We Can Know Whom We Have Believed.—The saved man has security—the peace that passeth all understanding, which no mortal can take away. This truth enables the believer to sing through his tears. This is an assurance that every believer can possess through the triumphant victory of our Lord over the grave. Paul said with positive assurance, "I know whom I have be-

lieved, and am persuaded that he is able to keep that
which I have committed unto him against that day" (2
Tim. 1:12). The greatest comfort that comes to a family
is in the Prince of peace. It is the presence of the Lord
that helps our faltering hearts today.

All Things Work Together for Good.—The tender
promise of Romans 8:28 seems to us a paradox at this
time of death. The Lord did not say that all things are
good but rather that "all things *work together* for good
to them that love God." Our Lord, who sympathizes
with us "like as a father pitieth his children" (Psalm 103:
13), is not saying to those whose hearts are bowed down
with grief that we should not regard this as a tragedy.
However, all the experiences of life can work together
to make us better and keep us from becoming bitter.

We Have a Body Not Made with Hands.—Even as our
houses are not made to withstand all storms, our bodies
are not made to withstand forever the ravages of life. In
sickness, pain, and death, we look to God for relief, for
we know that our God is "a very present help in trouble"
(Psalm 46:1). A time comes when we have to leave this
mortal body, "for this corruptible must put on incorrup-
tion, and this mortal must put on immortality" (1 Cor.
15:53). We know that this tabernacle of clay will one
day be dissolved, but we have the blessed assurance that
when "our earthly house of this tabernacle [is] dissolved,
we have a building of God, an house not made with
hands, eternal in the heavens" (2 Cor. 5:1).

There Is Comfort for the Sorrowing.—"Blessed be God,
even the Father of our Lord Jesus Christ, the Father of
mercies, and the God of all comfort; who comforteth

us in all our tribulation" (2 Cor. 1:3-4). We are assured of the abiding presence of God, for Jesus said, "The comforter, which is the Holy Ghost, whom the Father will send in my name, he shall teach you all things, and bring all things to your remembrance, whatsoever I have said unto you. Peace I leave with you, my peace I give unto you: not as the world giveth, give I unto you. Let not your heart be troubled, neither let it be afraid" (John 14:26-27).

Of all things that man knows, we know that Jesus is present with us today and weeps with us, even as he wept by the grave of his friend Lazarus in those days gone by.

3

Heaven's View of Death

Philippians 1:21

To say farewell is one of the hardest tasks of life. Parting from our loved ones for a brief period brings momentary sadness. When we face the finality of death, it always brings to our hearts the deepest shadows of sorrow. But we must not think of physical death as parting forever. This is not the Christian concept, for the Bible teaches that there shall be a glad reunion some day.

It is difficult indeed for us to think of the passing of the young without thinking in terms of tragedy. It would seem that in the normal span of time there would be so many days left. But there is no day that is certain; there is no year that is promised. The Scriptures say, "Remember now thy Creator in the days of thy youth" (Eccl. 12:1). James wrote, "Whereas ye know not what shall be on the morrow. For what is your life? It is even a vapour, that appeareth for a little time, and then vanisheth away" (4:14). Life has no guarantee; it holds only uncertainties. Sir Walter Raleigh described life as a journey, while Shakespeare thought of it as a drama. Burke called it a shadow. Job said, "Now my days are swifter than a post" (9:25).

It is the natural thinking of all that we will live to old age. But in the reality of life this is not always true. Is it biblical that we should view the death of the young as a tragedy? Should we not realize that "to die is gain" at any age? Heaven is the destined abiding-place of every Christian. Should we not realize that when it is dark here, the sun is shining elsewhere? Should we not remind ourselves that when the ship leaves the harbor it is enroute to some other shore? As Christians, we can know that even though this earthly house is destroyed, a building eternal is waiting in heaven. Listen to John L. Mc-Creery's "There Is No Death."

> There is no death! The stars go down
>   To rise upon some other shore,
> And bright in heaven's jeweled crown
>   They shine forevermore.
>
> There is no death! An angel form
>   Walks o'er the earth with silent tread;
> He bears our best loved things away,
>   And then we call them "dead."
>
> He leaves our hearts all desolate—
>   He plucks our fairest, sweetest flowers;
> Transplanted into bliss, they now
>   Adorn immortal bowers.

Death Is Not the End.—Death is not the end but the beginning. For the Christian it is life instead of death. Life does not die. Our physical body sleeps until the resurrection, but our spirit goes home to God who gave it. One has written, "Death is not only the real beginning of life; it is the beginning of real life." "To live is Christ," declared Paul, "and to die is to continue to be with Christ." This is the continued relationship of which Paul was speaking. His only problem, being "in a strait betwixt two," was that "to abide in the flesh is more needful for you" (Phil. 1:23-24).

It is well with the believer whatever the choice of providence. If he stays in the flesh, he is in Christ's work and with Christ's friends. If he dies, he is with Christ. Either way he is with Christ; only the circumstances around him are changed. Paul's perplexity came from his passion for the people that he served. He knew full well that the choice was really up to God and this he accepted without murmur.

Our young friend here, it seems, was just beginning to live. Yet it is far better to live on heaven's side than it is here. No Christian would really want to live forever in this life with all its imperfections. The best is yet to be! Martha said to Jesus, "If thou hadst been here, my brother had not died." Jesus answered her, "I am the resurrection, and the life: he that believeth in me, though he were dead, yet shall he live: and whosoever liveth and believeth in me shall never die. Believest thou this?" (John 11:25-26).

Death Is Not Loss.—Death is not loss but gain for the Christian. "To die is gain," Paul said. Let us cease thinking that it is a pity to receive a promotion from the Lord. Here everything is transient; in heaven everything is permanent. On earth we know only man's guesses; in heaven we possess God's complete revelation. The invitation of our Lord to his friend was, "Come ye blessed, inherit the kingdom." This was Paul's confidence in the Lord. "To depart," according to one scholar, is from the Greek word used concerning "loosing the ship from its moorings" or "striking one's tent." Paul said, "We know that if our earthly house of this tabernacle were dissolved, we have a building of God, an house not made with hands, eternal in the heavens" (2 Cor. 5:1). Ella Wheeler Wilcox has given to the world her testimony concerning "Faith."

> I will no doubt, though all my ships at sea
>   Come drifting home with broken masts and sails;
>   I shall believe the Hand which never fails,
> From seeming evil worketh good to me;
>   And, though I weep because those sails are battered,
>   Still will I cry, while my best hopes lie shattered,
>   "I trust in Thee."

We rehearse the words of the Apostle to the Gentiles, who said, "We know that all things work together for good to them that love God" (Rom. 8:28). The Bible has not said that all things are good but that in our submissive hearts they can work good in our lives.

Death Is Not Defeat.—Death is not defeat; it is victory. "O death, where is thy sting? O grave, where is thy victory?" (1 Cor. 15:55). Victory has been the triumph word of the New Testament, since Jesus became "the firstfruits of them that slept." We know that death cannot hold our bodies forever prisoner. "The Lord himself shall descend from heaven with a shout," we are told, "with the voice of the archangel, and with the trump of God: and the dead in Christ shall rise first" (1 Thess. 4:16). We are encouraged to comfort one another with these words. How can death be defeat when our loved one is already with Christ? How can it be anything but victory when the physical body has been laid down to receive the celestial gift of God? It is victory now!

"We know that, when he shall appear, we shall be like him; for we shall see him as he is" (1 John 3:2). This is our victory, even our faith! "Thanks be to God, which giveth us the victory through our Lord Jesus Christ" (1 Cor. 15:57).

4

Loose Him and Let Him Go

John 11:18-45

There came a time in Paul's experience when with resignation he said, "I am now ready to be offered, and the time of my departure is at hand" (2 Tim. 4:6). Long, lingering illness makes many a saint of God anxious for that great departure.

The suffering of pain is older than Job. Indeed, the problem of human suffering is as old as human life itself. "Why all of this suffering?" is the question of many aching hearts. To all, suffering seems to be so needless. However, life teaches that we learn from our sufferings as well as from our joys.

Suffering will hearten some and harden others. Paul wanted to know Christ more completely, for he cried out from his soul, "That I may know him . . . and the fellowship of his sufferings" (Phil. 3:10). "Surely he hath borne our griefs, and carried our sorrows," prophesied Isaiah, "yet we did esteem him stricken, smitten of God, and afflicted. But he was wounded for our transgressions, he was bruised for our iniquities: the chastisement of our peace was upon him; and with his stripes we are healed" (53:4-5). We have been assured by Simon Peter that God will, "after that ye have suffered a while, make you perfect, stablish, strengthen, settle you" (1 Peter 5:10).

We have assurance in the Lamentations of Jeremiah that "the Lord will not cast off for ever: but though he cause grief, yet will he have compassion according to the multitude of his mercies. For he doth not afflict willingly nor grieve the children of men" (3:31-33). The apostle Paul also said that "our light affliction, which is but for a moment, worketh for us a far more exceeding and eternal weight of glory" (2 Cor. 4:17). In the great eighth chapter of Romans, he continued, "for I reckon that the sufferings of this present time are not worthy to be compared with the glory which shall be revealed in us" (8:18).

Sufferings purify the saint of God and make him know that the finality of death holds no peril for him. An unknown author has phrased it:

> Rocks and storms I will fear no more,
> When on that eternal shore;
> Drop the anchor, furl the sail!
> I am safe within the veil.

What possible good can come from suffering? It can strengthen the faith. We learn from the saints of God who are facing the "swelling of the Jordan" that there is no fear in the mystery of the valley of death. We learn how to die from those great Christians whom we have watched die victoriously in the faith.

"Loose Him."—Jesus stood by the grave of Lazarus and "cried with a loud voice, Lazarus, come forth" (John 11:43). Then he instructed those who stood by to loose him from the burial clothes. The Great Physician has stood in the shadows of the bedside each day of this terminal illness. He, of compassionate mercy, quietly spoke to the angels to come for this one and "loose him" from the frailties of the flesh. The psalmist prayed, "Lord, make me to know mine end, and the measure of my days, what it is; that I may know how frail I am" (39:4).

This loved one has been loosed from the frailties of the flesh and from the burdens that bound his heart down here. Where there has been sickness, there is now joy. Where there has been pain, there is now relief. Where there has been dread, there is now victory. The perils of sudden death do not come to him that suffers and has opportunity to make total preparation for this passage. From out of God's Word there comes the prayer, "Let me die the death of the righteous, and let my last end be like his!" (Num. 23:10).

Death is always difficult for the loved ones, but the suffering of this precious one helps us in our hearts to pray, "Loose him." When there is sickness in the home, we forget our own health and live for the sake of others. We watch over them, toil for them, and would die for them. Would we then sorrow as one who has no hope? Would we grieve when their best good and highest happiness calls them from us? We would not bring them back to this place of suffering when we know they are at home with God. George Washington Bethune has said,

It is not death to die,
  To leave this weary road,
And, midst the brotherhood on high,
  To be at home with God.

"Let Him Go."—It has been said, "Faith grows a Christian, life proves a Christian, toil confirms a Christian, and death crowns a Christian!" This beloved one who suffered so patiently has gone to his eternal resting place. A lingering illness was able to inflict its worst on this temporary body in which he dwelt, but it could never touch his triumphant spirit. Our dwelling here is meant to be transient. It is only temporary at best and little more than threescore and ten at most.

When Jesus came to Bethany, Martha said to her sister Mary, "The Master is come, and calleth for thee" (John 11:28). In this hour he comes to us and calls to us. He comes to commune, to console, and to comfort. He comes to set free our loved one who has been cabined for this long while in a pain-wracked body.

The Lord has come to "loose him, and let him go" (John 11:44) to the reunion in glory. What a glad day that must have been when he joined again those he had "loved and lost a while." He now enjoys the permanent peace and the eternal blessing of the chosen of God of all ages. Truly he rejoices with the psalmist: "Precious in the sight of the Lord is the death of his saints. O Lord, truly I am thy servant; I am thy servant, and the son of thine handmaid: thou hast loosed my bonds" (116:15-16).

The firmness of his faith did not falter, even though

he lived under the shadow of death for these many months. His answer was much the same as that of John Quincy Adams when he was asked, in his eightieth year, how he was. He replied, "I am quite well, but the house is worn out." His faith assured him "that if our earthly house of this tabernacle were dissolved, we have a building of God, an house not made with hands, eternal in the heavens" (2 Cor. 5:1).

And where has he gone? He has gone home to our Father who hears and answers prayer. The Lord heard the prayer to be relieved of this body with its pain, to take away this disease that has no healing, to be given a new body that knows no imperfections, to go to a new city that knows no sickness or death. Triumphantly, we know that the Lord has the last word and that the grave holds no final victory; we are assured that our "labour is not in vain in the Lord" (1 Cor. 15:58).

5

Our Life Beyond

1 Corinthians 15:42-58

Never has immortality meant so much to us as it does on an occasion such as this. Paul, in the great resurrection chapter, said that Jesus brought life and immortality to light. In the gloom of grief we search anxiously for the gleam of God's love. We have been reminded at the Christmas season of the great gift of his Son. At Easter time we have recalled that when the stone was rolled away, light dispelled the darkness of the tomb. But only when sorrow comes so suddenly do we comprehend the blessed fulness of eternal life. We know that the writer of Hebrews has said, "It is appointed unto men once to die" (9:27). This has seemed harsh, but it is fully evidenced now.

With softened voices, we ask with the same anxious concern that has lasted for countless centuries, "If a man die, will he live again?" That age-old question of Job is in our hearts today. We reverently peer into the unknown with Job, also, when he says, "But man dieth, and wasteth away: yea, man giveth up the ghost, and where is he?" (Job 14:10).

31

There have been many answers given concerning the place of the dead. The materialist says the dead are nowhere. "Earth to earth, ashes to ashes, dust to dust"—that is all! Though we have come in our generation to a near-worship of science, we find it strangely silent concerning immortality. William Oxler of Oxford has said, "Science knows temporal; spiritual is not temporal."

America's most eloquent agnostic, Robert Ingersoll, could give no more hope at the grave of a little child than to say, "Why do we fear that which will come to all? We do not know which is better, life or death; or whether the light here is somewhere else on the dawn . . . every coffin asks us whither."

But Jesus affirmed, "I am the resurrection, and the life: he that believeth in me, though he were dead, yet shall he live: And whosoever liveth and believeth in me shall never die" (John 11:25-26). Today, as our faith searches for a firm foundation, we realize that "the way that seemeth right unto man" is not enough for sorrowing and aching hearts.

We would turn to God for a positive hope. Does the Word of God have a message for us? The Bible declares: "For this say we unto you by the Word of the Lord."

Continuity of Life.—Jesus said, "I am [now] the God of Abraham, Isaac, and Jacob." He is the God of the living and our beloved dead are now in the land of eternally living ones.

Alfred Lord Tennyson was said to have been asked to write down his thoughts concerning death when he returned from the funeral of a friend. It was then that he wrote "Crossing the Bar."

Sunset and evening star,
   And one clear call for me!
And may there be no moaning of the bar
   When I put out to sea.

But such a tide as moving seems asleep,
   Too full for sound and foam,
When that which drew from out the boundless deep
   Turns again home.

Twilight and evening bell,
   And after that the dark!
And may there be no sadness of farewell,
   When I embark.

For tho' from out our bourne of Time and Place
   The flood may bear me far,
I hope to see my Pilot face to face
   When I have crossed the bar.

Our friend has been for many years a beloved citizen of this city and now for eternity is a citizen of the Celestial City of God. The body is placed tenderly in the dust of the earth to await the trumpet of God at the resurrection morning. But the spirit has gone home to God who gave it.

There is no halfway place for the believer. There is no intermediate state, no period of soul-sleep, no purgatory. The Bible says we are alive in this body and then go out of this body into the presence of the Lord. The Bible teaches continuity of life. The heavens were opened and received the martyr Stephen when he cried out, "Lord Jesus, receive my spirit." Continuity of life was promised when Jesus said to the thief on the cross, "Verily I say unto thee, Today shalt thou be with me in paradise" (Luke 23:43).

Permanence of Personality.—Jesus never lost sight of the individual. Every child, every person, was of supreme importance to the Master. He died for everyone. He said, "I am come that they might have life, and that they might have it more abundantly" (John 10:10). When someone asked the great preacher, D. L. Moody, if we would know each other in heaven, he replied simply, "Don't you think we will have as much sense in heaven as we have here?"

There is remarkable evidence in the Bible of recognition after death. Jesus was recognized some eleven times after his death. The saints that were resurrected after the crucifixion were recognized by their loved ones (cf. Matt. 27:52-53). Moses and Elijah were recognized by Peter, James, and John on the mount of transfiguration. Paul declared, "Now I know in part; but then shall I know even as also I am known" (1 Cor. 13:12).

Conditions "Far Better."—Being human, we cannot help but think of ourselves today. We feel our loss, our separation, our loneliness, our sorrow. It will comfort our hearts to think of them, for the Word says that to be with the eternal Christ defies comparison. It is natural for us to want our loved ones to linger with us. It is Christian to commit them to his better hand. It takes great strength to pray sincerely as did Job, "The Lord gave, and the Lord hath taken away; blessed be the name of the Lord" (1:21).

We can pray this only when we are comforted by the

sure knowledge of our loved one's better existence. "Eye hath not seen, nor ear heard, neither have entered into the heart of man, the things which God hath prepared for them that love him" (1 Cor. 2:9).

Thus we say to our own hearts, "Thanks be to God, which giveth us the victory through our Lord Jesus Christ. Therefore, my beloved brethren, be ye stedfast, unmoveable, always abounding in the work of the Lord, forasmuch as ye know that your labour is not in vain in the Lord" (1 Cor. 15:57-58). Paul said he had "a desire to depart, and to be with Christ; which is far better" (Phil. 1:23).

6

Blessed Is the Man

Psalm 1:1-6

It is one thing to be lonely; it is an entirely different thing to be alone. You are strangely lonely in this sorrow, for it is your first time to experience shadows without your earthly father to lean on. Though you are lonely, you are not alone. The faith of your father and that of your own experience reveals to you the presence of your Heavenly Father.

It is a divine inspiration to realize that our tears are only tears of temporary separation. You cannot help but have mixed emotions today, for it is not all sorrow. There has been separation here, but there is a glad reunion in heaven for this one and your loved one who has gone before. Let there be no misconception about a Christian's death: "To live is Christ, and to die is gain," always, for the believer. This one would have found his emotions as the apostle Paul's:

"I am in a strait betwixt two, having a desire to depart, and to be with Christ; which is far better: nevertheless to abide in the flesh is more needful for you" (Phil. 1:23-24).

36

Knowledge of his family's need for him was the only thing that eased his homesickness for heaven. You know that heaven is better for him, even as you know also that it will be lonely for you here without him. Words never come easily when we share the sorrow of a family and try to describe the memory of a cherished friend.

Man.—He has written his own epitaph before our eyes. All the days of his manhood have been in this community. For thirty-seven years he worked for one railroad company before he retired. His workmen bear witness today that he was a man. President James A. Garfield said, "I intend to make myself a man and if I succeed in that, I shall succeed in everything." The greatest evidence of manliness is not in muscles but in maturity of character. Milton, in *Paradise Lost*, let God describe the creation of man in his own image,

> I made him just and right,
> Sufficient to have stood, though free to fall.

Our friend stood, and "blessed is the man" who stands for the right thing. Some men stand in the right way, while others just block the right-of-way. The psalmist described such a man as being a tall tree, a tower of strength, whose influence brings shade and comfort to those who come near. A Texas rancher aptly and beautifully described his father as being a "hitching post— someone to tie to."

Marriage.—We cannot think of this friend without thinking of his home. His family was the pride of his life. They were a closely knit group, and his epitaph would surely be, "He was a family man." Death separated the marriage partners of forty-two years four years ago. His sons were his joys and his prized possessions. "Blessed is the man," indeed, of whom it can be said that all his sons followed him as he followed Christ and today are active church members. He leaves unto them "a good name" which is "rather to be chosen than great riches" (Prov. 22:1). His example was meaningful to his children as they follow his footsteps. "Train up a child in the way he should go: and when he is old, he will not depart from it" (Prov. 22:6).

All who knew him understood the devotion and delight that his grandchildren brought him. His children and grandchildren alike sensed his devotion to the Lord. As God spoke of Abraham, even so we speak of this father: "For I know him, that he will command his children and his household after him, and they shall keep the way of the Lord, to do justice and judgment" (Gen. 18:19).

Meaning.—Life was meaningful to this snowy-haired friend, for he understood the meaning of life. He who was "come that they might have life, and that they might have it more abundantly" (John 10:10) was the source of his strength. His faith in God gave him assurance of eternal life, and the thought of death brought no fear to him. His threescore and seven years had brought him many responsibilities but none that he shirked. His jolly humor was helpful to us all.

Some years ago he retired from his job, but he never retired from the Lord's service. His constant presence and support left no doubt in the minds of any concerning his devotion to God. His friends and neighbors knew of his intense loyalty to the church and of his love for the things that are right.

Life, to be truly meaningful, must have a goal. It can be said today of Mr. Harris, as was written in Numbers 21:11, that he "journeyed . . . toward the sunrising." Blessed is that man whose steps honor the Lord, whose children honor him, whose neighbors believe in him, whose friends respect him, and whose church will greatly miss him. The lingering influence of his life points us to the glorious sunrise of his entrance into heaven.

*This message was prepared for a faithful
Sunday school teacher of many years, Mrs.
B. W. Green of Fort Worth.*

7

Spiritual Statistics

Psalm 23:6

Dr. Clarence Macartney painted a beautiful word picture when he said, "God has placed in the hand of man two wonderful lamps. One is the lamp of hope, which leads us forward through the uncertain mists of the future; the other is the lamp of memory, which takes us by the hand and leads us through the mists of the past to the happy scenes and memories of yesterday."

Memory is a gift of God and can be a very beautiful thing. We would remind you of that which you already know. You have precious memories to last another lifetime, and the Scriptures say, "The memory of the just is blessed" (Prov. 10:7).

Memories furnish such clear pictures to the mind that words seem unnecessary. Mrs. Green's autobiography has been written so vividly that she does not need a eulogy. However, to eulogize this life would be to glorify Christ, for she has gained his eternal presence. Only we have suffered loss.

The declaration of her lifelong faith has been, "Surely

goodness and mercy shall follow me all the days of my life: and I will dwell in the house of the Lord for ever" (Psalm 23:6).

Numbers would serve almost as well as words to portray this woman, for the statistics of her noble life are inspiring.

84 Years of Life.—Beyond the "threescore and ten" years, this Christian lady has been our friend and neighbor. She had the enthusiastic energy of lesser years and remained interested in all the things about her, particularly in her family and in her church. She observed the commandment of promise and was rewarded with long life.

"The hoary head is a crown of glory, if it be found in the way of righteousness," declared the ancient sage (Prov. 16:31). The years gave to Mrs. Green poise, dignity, and experience; and to these were added the virtues of patience, love, and kindness. Methuselah existed for many years longer than any other man, but there is no evidence that he really knew of what life consisted or that he in any way followed his mighty father Enoch, who walked with God. This one lived up to the limits of her life. She wore out her earthly tabernacle in making glorious contributions to the kingdom of God.

66 Years of Marriage.—At her passing, Mrs. Green was the oldest mother in our church family. Until the passing of her husband, two years ago, their marriage was the longest. In these days of unstable homes this was an example that was meaningful to this church and community and was a blessing in the kingdom of God.

She had a way of saying, "I am eight times a millionaire

—I have eight children." Her family would testify that Proverbs 31 comes nearer describing their mother than anyone they know:

Strength and honour are her clothing; and she shall rejoice in time to come. She openeth her mouth with wisdom; and in her tongue is the law of kindness. She looketh well to the ways of her household, and eateth not the bread of idleness. Her children arise up, and call her blessed; her husband also, and he praiseth her. Many daughters have done virtuously, but thou excellest them all. Favour is deceitful, and beauty is vain. but a woman that feareth the Lord, she shall be praised. Give her of the fruit of her hands; and let her own works praise her in the gates (25-31).

Some have suggested that in these days of sickness, since her husband passed away, Mrs. Green gave up. Such a hearty Christian pioneer would never give up; she just simply wore out.

44 Years a Member of This Church.—The Green family moved to this community in 1917. On their very first Sunday here, they joined the Rosen Heights Baptist Church. It would be impossible to write the history of this great congregation without mentioning again and again this noble woman. She has made a marvelous contribution to the kingdom, for much in this church represents her prayers and toil and dedication. The Master has said, "Of such is the kingdom of heaven." This church has grown because of the sacrifices of such people.

Early in life, Mrs. Green realized that her life would last longer in her home and in her church than anywhere else, for these are the divine institutions of the Lord. May her tribe, "the salt of the earth" variety, increase! The kingdom has been extended because such people have lived and served without thought of credit or reward but with hearts full of love for the Lord.

33 Years a Teacher of One Class.—All of her mature years she has been a teacher in the Sunday school in the church of which she was a member. For many years she taught in the youth departments, but in the passing of time she became a teacher of the older ladies class and remained in that responsibility until she "went home." This record of thirty-three years is a wonderful testimony and gives insight into her spiritual stability. These long years represent the hot and the cold, the good and the bad, the ups and the downs of Sunday school work, week by week; yet she purposefully plodded on.

To Mrs. Green, teaching was thrilling. God gave her the gift of teaching. She was not satisfied with teaching just facts, nor did the mere teaching of lessons satisfy her. She taught life itself!

A writer has suggested that there are three types of teachers—the forgotten, the forgiven, and the remembered. The members of this class who are not already in heaven follow her reverently today to her last resting place. This they do, for indeed she has shared the winters of their lives and the joys of their summers. Through the years they have followed her, for she followed the teachings of the Master Teacher who came from God, even Jesus her Saviour. The emphases of her lessons became characteristics of her life.

A great educator once said concerning teachers, "One day one of your pupils will say, 'I remember one thing that you taught me.' " As Mrs. Green's pastor, I remember the consistent, Christian lessons that she taught, but I remember her deeds as well. One of these I especially treasure. I remember that she sat with my mother, who was a member of her class, the night my father went away. This one thing is chiseled in that part of a man that does not decay with the passing of time. We would crown with glory such a life and we say with reverent emotion, "Precious in the sight of the Lord is the death of [this one of] his saints" (Psalm 116:15).

To family and friends alike we say, "Therefore, brethren, stand fast, and hold the traditions which ye have been taught, whether by word, or our epistle" (2 Thess. 2:15).

No epitaph of ours could be more meaningful than these simple verses written by Lucille Ferguson, one of her daughters:

> The memories of my mother
> Are the sweetest thoughts I know;
> They fill my life with sunshine
> And make my pathway glow.
>
> The wisdom of her teaching
> Has helped me find the way
> To be a kinder person
> In all I do or say.

This message was prepared for an aged Christian whose life was consistent all his years for the glory of Christ.

8

Glimpses of Glory

2 Corinthians 12:2-4

The emotions of a saint in heaven are recorded in the words of the psalmist, "In thy presence is fulness of joy" (16:11). The apostle Paul, caught up into that perfect paradise, revealed that he had heard unspeakable words concerning the glory of God. He related, "I knew a man in Christ above fourteen years ago, (whether in the body, I cannot tell; or whether out of the body, I cannot tell: God knoweth;) such an one caught up to the third heaven. And I knew such a man, (whether in the body, or out of the body, I cannot tell: God knoweth;) how that he was caught up into paradise, and heard unspeakable words, which it is not lawful for a man to utter" (2 Cor. 12:2-4).

Our departed loved one has already exchanged this pall of gloom for the great glory of God. The sacred Scriptures have promised, "In the morning, then ye shall see the glory of the Lord" (Ex. 16:7). This precious promise dispels the darkness of the dungeon of death through which we are all called to pass.

45

The gospel hymn writer has exclaimed, concerning reunion with the Lord, "Oh, that will be glory for me!" We may speak of the glories of our native land, but how can this compare to heaven? Our great choirs have inspired us, but who would not prefer to hear the heavenly angels sing? The theme of all heaven is "blessing, and honour, and glory, and power, be unto him that sitteth upon the throne, and unto the Lamb for ever and ever" (Rev. 5:13).

When we are at last caught up with Paul to hear and see these unspeakable things, we shall for the first time understand the full meaning of Isaiah when he said, "Holy, holy, holy, is the Lord of hosts: the whole earth is full of his glory" (6:3). We must come with confident faith in the face of sorrow and know that death has not dispelled the glory of God. "The sufferings of this present time are not worthy to be compared with the glory which shall be revealed in us" (Rom. 8:18).

The Crown of Glory.—The Bible speaks concerning the crown of glory. Proverbs reminds us that "the hoary head is a crown of glory, if it be found in the way of righteousness" (16:31). The divinely inspired writer of this ancient book reflected that wisdom came with experience. He is reminding us that there is no greater testimony than the aged one with hair of snow telling us, "All the way my Saviour leads me, what have I to ask beside?" The hoary head testifies of toil and of triumphs; it reminds us of sickness and suffering. The white hair also reveals to us that the years are slipping silently by.

The testimony of an aged one who has been faithful to the Lord is the greatest prize of Christendom, for

Satan has no happy old men. Surely the Lord has heard the prayer of this one as he heard the prayer of the psalmist: "Cast me not off in the time of old age; forsake me not when my strength faileth" (71:9). God has promised never to leave or forsake his children. Isaiah was inspired to write, "Even to your old age I am he; and even to hoar hairs will I carry you: I have made, and I will bear; even I will carry, and will deliver you" (46:4).

The reward of faithfulness is, "Well done, thou good and faithful servant: thou hast been faithful over a few things, I will make thee ruler over many things: enter thou into the joy of thy lord" (Matt. 25:21). Faithfulness is our crowning glory, for he has encouraged us by saying, "Occupy until I come." Our friend has been faithful to his place of service in the church as was the wonderful apostle Paul. Paul longed for that crown of glory as he bared his heart in the dark dungeon of Rome and prepared his own funeral eulogy.

That consistent Christian committed himself to the Lord by saying, "I am now ready to be offered, and the time of my departure is at hand. I have fought a good fight, I have finished my course. I have kept the faith: Henceforth there is laid up for me a crown of righteousness, which the Lord, the righteous judge, shall give me at that day: and not to me only, but unto all them also that love his appearing" (2 Tim. 4:6-8).

The Place of Glory.—We are confident that "to be absent from the body" is "to be present with the Lord" (2 Cor. 5:8). To be in the eternal abiding place of God will indeed be eternal glory. Heaven is where God is. It defies the descriptions of men because most of that which exists on earth will be barred from its celestial doors. Grief and gloom will be shut out by the Great Physician. "God shall wipe away all tears from their eyes; and there shall be no more death, neither sorrow, nor crying, neither shall there be any more pain: for the former things are passed away" (Rev. 21:4). There will be no darkness because God himself will be our light. The day and night shall not be separated, for time shall cease to be.

No longer will we be tested, tried, troubled, or tired, for "there remaineth therefore a rest to the people of God" (Heb. 4:9). Kipling has partially pictured it in "L'Envoi":

When Earth's last picture is painted, and the tubes are twisted and dried,
When the oldest colors have faded, and the youngest critic has died,
We shall rest, and, faith, we shall need it—lie down for an aeon or two,
Till the Master of All Good Workmen shall put us to work anew.

And those that were good shall be happy; they shall sit in a golden chair;
They shall splash at a ten-league canvas with brushes of comets' hair;
They shall find real saints to draw from—Magdalene, Peter, and Paul;
They shall work for an age at a sitting, and never be tired at all!

And only the Master shall praise us, and only the Master shall blame;

And no one shall work for money, and no one shall work for
    fame;
But each for the joy of the working, and each, in his separate
    star,
Shall draw the Thing as he sees It for the God of Things as
    They are!

The Hope of Glory.—Can we be sure and steadfast in our hope of heaven? Paul wrote, "I would not have you to be ignorant, brethren, concerning them which are asleep, that ye sorrow not, even as others which have no hope" (1 Thess. 4:13). Our hope of glory is our belief in the Lord Jesus Christ as our personal Saviour. We are reassured by our faith in the hour of sorrow because we know that our departed loved one committed himself to the Lord many years ago.

He constantly testified of his hope in glory: "I know whom I have believed, and am persuaded that he is able to keep that which I have committed unto him against that day" (2 Tim. 1:12). And he could sing that old hymn by Edward Mote:

> My hope is built on nothing less
> Than Jesus' blood and righteousness.

The writer of the precious book of Hebrews reveals to us that the Christian's hope is "a strong consolation" to those "who have fled for refuge" (6:18). In the next verse the writer calls it the "hope we have as an anchor of the soul, both sure and stedfast" (6:19). Our hope is a person, "even Jesus" (6:20).

Our blessed Saviour knew that death, the final foe, would attack our lives. He prepared his disciples by saying to them, and to us: "Let not your heart be troubled: ye believe in God, believe also in me. In my Father's house are many mansions: if it were not so, I would have told you. I go to prepare a place for you. And if I go and prepare a place for you, I will come again, and receive you unto myself; that where I am, there ye may be also" (John 14:1-3).

Even as Paul heard that which is unspeakable, in this hour the spirit of the Lord would comfort you with his presence which is indescribable, "Christ in you, the hope of glory" (Col. 1:27).

Our friend could surely have said with the aged Simeon of long years ago, "Lord, now lettest thou thy servant depart in peace, according to thy word: for mine eyes have seen thy salvation" (Luke 2:29-30).

This message was prepared for a wonderful Christian mother, Mrs. W. I. Cannaday of Floydada, Texas.

9

Christ's Conqueror

Romans 8:37

Mrs. Cannaday would surely be thought of as one of the first ladies of our community because of her continued service. Jesus said, "Whosoever will be chief among you, let him be your servant" (Matt. 20:27). It was her joy and delight to serve others. She counted it a high privilege to be a servant of our Lord.

When one has been so faithful and active, it is difficult for us to think of her as being old. She never meant to let age make any difference; she never intended to "slack off." So often she would say, "When my days of service are over, I want to go home." Retirement held no lure for her. In her kind, dedicated way she would not be shelved. Her service was continuous from early youth until her sudden passing.

Three words would help to characterize this gracious lady—Christian, cheerful, and courageous.

Christian.—A passage from the writings of Paul to young Timothy reads, "Now the end of the commandment is charity out of a pure heart, and of a good con-

51

science, and of faith unfeigned" (1 Tim. 1:5). It would be impossible to write an epitaph of this one without using the words love, faith, home, and church. She was queenly in these realms, which is the highest epitaph that anyone could lay at the feet of a mother. "Her children arise up, and call her blessed" (Prov. 31:28).

Her father was a pioneer minister, so she was reared in a Christian home. This community has witnessed her life from the time she came as a young bride until snow sprinkled her hair in her seventy-seventh year. Along with her family, she was able to adjust to the demands of the frontier when the conveniences of ranch life were few. She and that marvelous generation of which she was a part did so much to make our community what it is.

Being a Christian, she sought the fellowship of the church of her Lord. She prayed and worked that it might develop. The church minutes of this congregation eloquently testify to the respect that the members have had for her Christian life. The records reveal that she has been on every building committee that our congregation has had. A progressive pioneer, indeed. Only a few hours before her homegoing, she spoke concerning her interest in the building committee work.

Cheerful.—Few families have known as much sickness as has this family. Cheerfully, quietly, and in the spirit of the Great Physician, she waited upon those of her own household. Never was she one to feel that her burdens were too many. Rather, she sought out others to help. Her attitude of cheerfulness was a constant encouragement to those in need. Quietly she moved among those less fortunate, helping here and touching there—leaving the breath of God wherever she went. She had learned the secret of "getting" through "giving," for as the Bible says, "Blessed be God, even the Father of our Lord Jesus Christ, the Father of mercies, and the God of all comfort; who comforteth us in all our tribulation, that we may be able to comfort them which are in any trouble, by the comfort wherewith we ourselves are comforted of God" (2 Cor. 1:3-4).

Courageous.—This Christian mother claimed the Lord's promise, "As I was with Moses, so I will be with thee: I will not fail thee, nor forsake thee. Be strong and of a good courage" (Josh. 1:5-6). She heeded the warning and encouragement of Jesus: "In the world ye shall have tribulation; but be of good cheer; I have overcome the world" (John 16:33).

One has written that "the best hearts are the bravest." Bravery may not come with the beat of a drum; rather, it may be in the very quietness of a mother who courageously cheers a feverish child in the wee hours of the morning. It also may be in the encouragement of another to go on when the burdens have become almost unbearably heavy. Joaquin Miller has put it in verse:

The greatest battle that ever was fought—
    Shall I tell you where and when?
On the maps of the world you will find it not:
    It was fought by the Mothers of Men.

Not with cannon or battle shot,
    With sword or nobler pen;
Not with eloquent word or thought
    From the wonderful minds of men;

But deep in a walled-up woman's heart,
  A woman that would not yield;
But bravely and patiently bore her part;
  Lo! there is the battlefield.

No marshalling troups, no bivouac song,
  No banner to gleam and wave;
But, Oh! these battles they last so long—
  From babyhood to the grave!

The Word of God says that "we walk by faith, not by sight" (2 Cor. 5:7). As Sydney Smith has said, "A great deal of talent is lost in this world for want of a little courage." Many years ago this friend, as a child, courageously committed her life into the tender hands of our Saviour. Because of this, not only was she able to conquer life but she has conquered in death, also. "Then shall be brought to pass the saying that is written, Death is swallowed up in victory. But thanks be to God, which giveth us the victory through our Lord Jesus Christ" (1 Cor. 15:54,57).

10

His Blessed Presence

Psalm 139:1-18

The psalmists understood the experiences of human heartache. The book of Psalms has always been a blessing and a benediction to God's people as they have "walked through the valley of the shadow" and through the very door of death itself.

The promise of our Master that he would never leave us nor forsake us was for time and eternity. Our Lord was with our friend in his earthly life, and he now has gone to be with the Lord in eternity. Death brings separation and separation brings sorrow, but our sorrow causes no doubt. "I would not have you to be ignorant, brethren, concerning them which are asleep," wrote the apostle Paul, "that ye sorrow not, even as others which have no hope" (1 Thess. 4:13). Jesus gave his disciples the words that dispelled their doubts and brought hope to them in the midst of their hopelessness.

Our hope is based on the assurance that our friend was saved by grace and that he had that blessed hope which is the precious promise of every Christian. As the hymn writer has said, "In times like these, we need a Saviour," because we know that human strength will not suffice. In the hour of sorrow, we look toward the sunlight of his love.

His Presence Gives Us Faith.—Knowing full well that such times would come to our hearts, the Master said, "I will pray the Father, and he shall give you another Comforter, that he may abide with you for ever; I will not leave you comfortless: I will come to you" (John 14:16,18). It is a blessed truth that he has promised not to leave us "as orphans." He does not desert us in the swelling of the Jordan. He never leaves us alone.

When sorrow causes our hearts to falter and faint, we remember again that "faith cometh by hearing, and hearing by the word of God" (Rom. 10:17). Looking unto Jesus, who is the author and finisher of our faith, we know that he is sitting at the right hand of God. We believe in the triumphant resurrection of our Saviour, as the Scripture says, "Now is Christ risen from the dead, and become the firstfruits of them that slept" (1 Cor. 15:20).

We walk by faith and not by sight, knowing that we do not leave this earth alone but in heavenly company. Jesus promised his disciples that he would come for them (John 14:3). There should be no fear in our hearts. We are not disturbed at the thought of meeting God, for Jesus said, "He who hath seen me hath seen the Father." The psalmist sang, "In thy presence is fulness of joy."

The examples that we find throughout this sacred book renew our faith. It tells of Enoch and Elijah's translation.

We have the record of the mighty Moses being cared for in his last moments only by the Lord. God continues to gather his children unto himself. "Precious in the sight of the Lord is the death of his saints" (Psalm 116:15).

His Presence Gives Us Fellowship.—Fellowship with God was very real to our friend. It will now continue uninterrupted and forever unbroken in God's presence. The fellowship of his family was sure and steadfast. The comforts and conveniences for his loved ones were goals of his life. His thoughtfulness was reciprocated by tender fellowship in his family circle. Even now in the halls of heaven there is reunion with that one who has gone before.

This friend loved the house of the Lord. The friends of the Lord were his friends. There is always joy in the reunion of the people of God. A great English clergyman wrote to a preacher friend, "I hope that in heaven our cottages are close together." The fellowship of our friends is meaningful to us because of that one who is the Friend of all friends, who "sticketh closer than a brother." He has promised that even though father, mother, sister, and brother forsake us, he will never leave us alone. Because of him we sing, "Blest be the tie that binds our hearts in Christian love."

His Presence Guarantees Our Future.—Jesus came down from heaven in order that we might go up to heaven. Words are hollow when we try to tell of the indescribable beauty of heaven. John was separated from his loved ones on the Isle of Patmos. He was looking forward to that day when he would never again know separation. The greatest glory of heaven is the presence of God. Wherever God is will be heaven for us. The divine presence of God abides with us here whether we are aware of it or not, but up there, never again will we be unconscious of it. Paul wrote: "I reckon that the sufferings of this present time are not worthy to be compared with the glory which shall be revealed in us" (Rom. 8:18).

D. L. Moody once said, "Heaven is a city without tears, a city without pain, without sorrow, without sickness, without death. Think of a place where temptation cannot come . . . think of a city that is not built with hands. Where the buildings do not grow old with time. Think of a city where hearses do not creep with their sad burdens to the cemetery; a city without graves or crypts, without sins or sorrow, without marriage or mournings, without births or burials. A city which glories in having Jesus as its King, angels for its guards and whose citizens are saints."

There is a beautiful saying modeled after the Beatitudes: "Blessed are they that are homesick for heaven: for they shall come home!" What is our future? There is a rest guaranteed: "There remaineth therefore a rest to the people of God" (Heb. 4:9). "Blessed are the dead which die in the Lord . . . they may rest from their labours; and their works do follow them" (Rev. 14:13). We are guaranteed by the promises of God that our earthly bodies will be resurrected. "The Lord himself shall descend from heaven with a shout, with the voice of the archangel, and with the trump of God: and the dead in Christ shall rise first" (1 Thess. 4:16).

The Lord has assured us that he will reward our faithfulness: "Well done, thou good and faithful servant . . . enter thou into the joy of thy Lord" (Matt. 25:21). What more would we desire to hear? We rejoice as much as human hearts will allow that our friend has already heard this glad welcome from his beloved Lord.

This message was prepared for an elderly man who was a faithful officer of the church and had a devoted family.

11

Our Father's House

John 14:1-9

John, the beloved disciple, exiled on the Isle of Patmos in his old age, wrote of a vision of heaven, "They heard a great voice from heaven saying unto them, Come up hither. And they ascended up to heaven in a cloud" (Rev. 11:12). Our beloved friend also heard the voice of God. He no longer needs our earthly comfort, for he is now in the very presence of God.

It is indeed a blessed truth to know that he who wept at the grave of Lazarus weeps with us today. In this sorrow, we turn to the Lord's Word for strength. The sacred Word encourages our faint hearts as it promises, "The last enemy that shall be destroyed is death. Then shall be brought to pass the saying that is written, Death is swallowed up in victory" (1 Cor. 15:26,54). It is true that physical death has come to his body, but our faithful friend has gone up higher, and is beyond the hurts of this earth.

Paul described this existence—up higher with Christ—as being "far better." The subject of heaven is always in season. It is the blessed state of mind and it is indeed "heavenly" to dwell upon it. The Bible assures us that it is a place as well, even the eternal dwelling place of our God. We do not know all that we would like to know today about heaven, but the Bible tells us all that we need to know. It is beyond description, beyond comparison. "Eye hath not seen, nor ear heard, neither have entered into the heart of man, the things which God hath prepared for them that love him" (1 Cor. 2:9). Human language is not sufficient to reveal what the King of kings has prepared for his children.

Separation.—When your loved one was separated from you, he was instantly separated unto Christ. You have gone often to your earthly father's house, and now your father has gone to his heavenly Father's house, "an house not made with hands, eternal in the heavens" (2 Cor. 5:1). For a while the tabernacle of the flesh will be laid away to await the bodily resurrection: "Then shall the dust return to the earth as it was: and the spirit shall return unto God who gave it" (Eccl. 12:7). This separation should hold no fear, for the Bible promises, "Behold, I shew you a mystery; We shall not all sleep, but we shall all be changed, In a moment, in the twinkling of an eye, at the last trump: for the trumpet shall sound, and the dead shall be raised incorruptible, and we shall be changed" (1 Cor. 15:51-52).

It is human for us to sorrow over the separation that has come, but our Lord provides divine comfort as we think rather upon the things to which our loved one has been separated. Already he has seen the angels for the first time. Already he has heard the angelic choirs sing.

Already he has been received into the bosom of the Father. Even now he walks among the patriarchs of the Bible. We weep because of our separation, but we rejoice that we have the hope of reunion with the loved ones who have gone before.

Heaven is not only a place of separation from this earth, it is a place of eternal security. Locked out is sickness, sorrow, pain, and death. Locked out forever are heartaches, frustrations, disappointments, disillusionment, and doubt. Secure indeed are the treasures of God. Jesus said it is a place "where neither moth nor rust doth corrupt, and where thieves do not break through nor steal" (Matt. 6:20). Only those enter there whose names are now written in the "Lamb's Book of Life."

Appreciation.—Only today, or in other times like these, we come to appreciate fully what God has prepared for us. Jesus said, "Let not your heart be troubled: ye believe in God, believe also in me. In my Father's house are many mansions: if it were not so, I would have told you. I go to prepare a place for you. And if I go and prepare a place for you, I will come again, and receive you unto myself; that where I am, there ye may be also" (John 14:1-3). It is a blessed truth to know that Jesus comes for his children. We do not walk toward our destination alone. He knows the way; he opened the grave and ascended into heaven.

To those who think only of our earthly cities of asphalt and cement, it is hard to realize what a wonderful place the Celestial City of God is. There we shall have perfect knowledge. "Now we see through a glass, darkly; but then face to face: now I know in part; but then shall I know even as also I am known" (1 Cor. 13:12). Jesus said, "I am the way, the truth, and the life." The shadows of night and darkness shall vanish away and we shall be complete and perfect. "Behold, what manner of love the Father hath bestowed upon us, that we should be called the sons of God: therefore the world knoweth us not, because it knew him not. Beloved, now are we the sons of God, and it doth not yet appear what we shall be: but we know that, when he shall appear, we shall be like him; for we shall see him as he is" (1 John 3:1-2). As the old hymn put it:

> We shall come with joy and gladness,
>   We shall gather round the throne;
> Face to face with those that love us,
>   We shall know as we are known:
> And the song of our redemption,
>   Shall resound through endless day,
> When the shadows have departed
>   And the mists have rolled away.
>
> We shall know as we are known,
>   Nevermore to walk alone,
> In the dawning of the morning
>   Of that bright and happy day:
> We shall know each other better,
>   When the mists have rolled away.

Glorification.—We are told that when those who have served in the ranks of the Salvation Army die, they are listed, not under the heading of "Deaths," but rather under "Promotions," as having been "promoted to glory." It is an abiding truth of God that to die is gain,

as Paul assured us in Philippians 1:21. Fannie Crosby has
phrased it so beautifully:

> Some day the silver cord will break
> And I no more as now shall sing;
> But, O, the joy when I shall wake
> Within the palace of the King!
>
> And I shall see Him face to face
> And tell the story—Saved by grace!

The apostle Paul longed for the "crown of righteousness, which the Lord, . . . shall give me at that day" (2
Tim. 4:8). God has surely rewarded this faithful one,
for he has said, "Thou hast been faithful over a few
things, I will make thee ruler over many things: enter
thou into the joy of thy Lord" (Matt. 25:21). "Ye shall
receive a crown of glory that fadeth not away," said the
apostle Peter to some of the early Christians (1 Peter
5:4).

The world would say to you today, "Weep not!" for
it has no other answer. When Jesus walked upon the
earth, he wept with those who mourned. In the book of
Revelation, God promises that when in our glorification
we go home to him, he "shall wipe away all tears from
[our] eyes; and there shall be no more death, neither sorrow, nor crying, neither shall there be any more pain: for
the former things are passed away" (Rev. 21:4). "The
toils of the road will seem nothing, when we get to the
end of the way."

This eulogy was delivered at the service of Alfred A. Brian, Jr., minister of education at Rosen Heights Baptist Church, Fort Worth.

12

"And Jesus . . . Loved Him"

Mark 10:21

In an interview with an outstanding young man, it is said that Jesus beheld him and loved him (cf. Mark 10). However, the similarity of the young ruler and Al Brian ends there. For in selfishness the young ruler turned away from Jesus, while with loving dedication, Al gave himself to the Saviour for time and for eternity.

To know Al was to love him. One had the feeling when meeting him that here was one of God's choice spirits. To know him was to be aware that he came to this church, not to be ministered unto, but to minister. He counted himself a servant, as the Lord said, "Whosoever will be great among you . . . shall be servant of all" (Mark 10:43-44). Wherever the opportunity was given, whatever the need, he did not know what it was to turn away from any chance to render a testimony for the Lord.

As we walk with the Lord through the Gospels, we come to that experience in the life of Jesus when he stood by the tomb of Lazarus. He was touched by the sorrow of Lazarus' family. Jesus realized that in a few minutes he would speak the word which would make Lazarus live again. Yet, the recognition that this thing called death was just for a moment's duration did not remove from him the feeling of great emotion. Those standing by said, "Behold, how he must have loved him." There were tears on the face of Jesus; it is recorded as the shortest verse in our Bible that "Jesus wept." By his journey back to Bethany and his presence at the tomb of Lazarus, it was obvious that he cared.

The comfort that abides with us, the thing which helps more than any other, is the fact that the Lord is in this experience with us. He cares for us as no one else can. This is the real reason why we can go on with our work.

Tribute.—Words are so desperately empty and unable to convey the real feeling of the soul, but there is a word of tribute which I would like to say when I think of Al Brian. Only twenty-seven years old, he was the first-born son in a parsonage home. A score and seven years seem so short, but few men have had the joy of being loved as devotedly as Al. And I would quickly say that few men, if any, have ever deserved it as much as he. Love begets love—when someone loves you, you love in return. Al shared, and because he shared, his sympathy and his love were returned.

His family was devoted to him—first his loving parents. Devoted indeed was his marvelous companion. Devoted was his church family to him. Happy was his relationship with the church staff. Especially was he loved by his pastor. Al knew the assurance of love about him and the ever-present love of his Heavenly Father. This wealth of love he shared, not with a few, but with people from all walks of life.

Yesterday morning an elderly lady slowed her steps to say in a quiet voice, "Lord, help us! Not Brother Brian!" Young men shook hands and shook their heads and went on without words. Little children asked for him—all of this because in his life there was love.

Time.—When we think of a successful life, we cannot think in terms of years and months and days. In Al's life, we think of acts and deeds and accomplishments. We think of his doing that which the Lord purposed for him to do. I suppose that for the first time many of us are really conscious of the fact that there was a divine sense of urgency about Al's mission in life. The foundation-stone of action for him was, "I must work while it is day, for the night cometh when no man shall work."

If the burden was heavy and a suggestion came that he should not do so much, he answered with a shrug of the shoulders and an air of "I must be about my Master's business." These pastors who have served with him, these young men who have sung with him, you who have loved him as your leader, you who have worshiped with him—all could give a word of testimony today that he was constantly about his Master's business.

Testimony.—If I could choose only one word to describe this friend, I would use the word "righteous." No other word would speak so much and say it so well. I have had the privilege of walking with him day by day. I think I knew him well, and I never knew Al to have an unchristian spirit.

His speech was always full of the things of the Lord. He was self-sacrificing and humble in spirit. He had a desire to serve others. He had a feeling of sympathy and was sensitive to the needs of others. His firm handshake, his ability to call everyone by name, gave each the feeling of being in the presence of one who actually cared about him and whose mission in life was to help.

Trust.—God endowed this young man with many abilities; his talents were several. But beyond this, he was absolutely trustworthy in the responsibilities that God put into his life. Few young men ever have the privilege of as many devoted friends and the respect of so many of his elders as Al did. This was not because of talent or position but because he was trustworthy. His family trusted him and his mother depended upon him. His wife trusted her heart and her love to him in unshaken confidence.

His teachers and officers followed him and they were never misled. His friends trusted him and they were rewarded with the freshness of his friendship. The heart of his pastor safely trusted in him. The last communication that I received from him was, "I am praying for you." To deserve and receive the trust of others is one of God's greatest blessings. Dinah Maria Craik has testified,

> Oh, the comfort—the inexpressible comfort
> of feeling safe with a person,
> Having neither to weigh thoughts,
> Nor measure words—but pouring them
> All right out—just as they are—
> Chaff and grain together—
> Certain that a faithful hand will

Take and sift them—
Keep what is worth keeping—
And with the breath of kindness
Blow the rest away.

Triumph.—Today we come to the test. There are some who say that this is tragedy. It would be easy for me to agree with you. But we must remember that this is not tragedy for Al but triumph! Al had the privilege of being led to the Lord by his preacher-father. He had the joy of being baptized by his father. He had the privilege of being married by his father. Now he is united with his father. When he graduated from school, I counted it a privilege to sit with his family. Sorrow came into his home, as sorrow came into ours, and each occasion of sorrow we shared together. These experiences brought a great closeness through the years.

As his pastor, I realize that though our hearts are heavy, and though this seems one of the saddest losses of our lives, it is still a great day for Al. We must never be so preoccupied with our own selfish sorrow that we would misunderstand for a moment that this is Al's coronation day. This is God's triumph in his life.

There is one Scripture passage that was particularly dear to Al. It was written on the flyleaf of the Bible which his brother gave him on the day of his ordination: "Wherefore seeing we also are compassed about with so great a cloud of witnesses, let us lay aside every weight, and the sin which doth so easily beset us, and let us run with patience the race that is set before us." Today that passage is completed for Al Brian, and this is his benediction: "Looking unto Jesus, the author and finisher of our faith" (Heb. 12:1-2).

For it is our Lord Jesus who says to him now, "Well done, thou good and faithful servant . . . enter thou into the joy of thy Lord" (Matt. 25:21).

This message was prepared for the Rev. L. H. Davis, pastor of Central Baptist Church of Fort Worth.

13

The Making of a Minister

John 14:1-10

Quietly, while Brother Davis worked at his desk, the Great Physician cured the illness which no earthly doctor could heal. At long last, he gave to Brother Davis the heavenly heartease. For some time our beloved friend had suffered from heart trouble, although he possessed all the while an untroubled heart.

The favorite passage of this minister was, "Let not your heart be troubled: ye believe in God, believe also in me. In my Father's house are many mansions: if it were not so, I would have told you" (John 14:1-2). Brother Davis believed this with all his heart, and it was the consoling message of his ministry.

As the prophet of old, Brother Davis had felt the divine calling: "He hath sent me . . . to comfort all that mourn" (Isa. 61:1-2). He visited frequently the sick, because he himself knew the confinement of illness. He knew the loneliness of the sickroom, although he himself was never alone. Jesus was as real to him as to any man I know. The spirit of Jesus was constantly exemplified by him. It was true of him as it was of the Master, that the common people heard him gladly. He sought no place of prominence. His only prayer was that he might have health and opportunity to serve. Where he served was not important—that he could serve meant everything.

Where there was a need, he went in the manner of the Good Samaritan. His brethren who observed his work could say concerning him, as was said of his Saviour, "He hath anointed [him] to preach the gospel to the poor; he hath sent [him] to heal the brokenhearted, to preach deliverance to the captives, and recovering of sight to the blind, to set at liberty them that are bruised, to preach the acceptable year of the Lord" (Luke 4:18-19).

Last Saturday evening when Brother Davis finished all the work on the new building and all preparation was made for the Lord's Day, all of the eyes of heaven were upon him as he sat down at his desk. Prophetically enough, his last words on the telephone to his wife were, "I am ready to go home." Before the family could come to him, the angels came and took him to his heavenly home.

Love.—The three great loves of his life were his Lord and the Lord's work, his wife and family, and his friends in the Lord, especially his preacher brethren. He loved preachers as do few men, and young ministers were always given a large place in his heart. He made every effort possible to help them and encourage them in the work. He was a good and useful man, even as Barnabas, who "was a good man, and full of the Holy Ghost and of faith" (Acts 11:24). Prior to his call to the ministry, he was active in his church and used his several talents for the Lord. He loved to sing and it was always a joy to hear him. Heaven was more real to us all as we felt his sure and steadfast faith when he sang, "I Won't Have to Cross Jordan Alone."

The love that he shared with his family was all that it ought to be. His wonderful wife for forty-two years was a loving comforter, helper, and mother. Often he said that the great love of God was even more real to him after he had experienced the love of his grandchildren.

Limit.—He used his energies and talents as much as it was possible to do. He often went beyond the limits of his physical endurance. With the apostle Paul he could truly say, "I magnify mine office" (Rom. 11:13). He believed that no man's life consisted in the abundance of things which he possessed, and he felt that real life was composed of opportunities for service.

This noble pastor was in a building program in each of the churches where he served throughout his ministry. Hardly was one completed until there was the call for another. Those calls in the night, such as Paul experienced, came to him: "Come over . . . and help us," and they never went unheeded. Surely the words of James Montgomery's poem titled "Well Done," could be said to Brother Davis:

> Servant of God, well done!
>   Rest from thy loved employ:
> The battle fought, the victory won,
>   Enter thy Master's joy.
>
> The pains of death are past,
>   Labour and sorrow cease,

> And Life's long warfare closed at last,
> Thy soul is found in peace.

Leave.—And now he has taken leave from us. His favorite passage, that precious promise of Jesus that he believed, has now been experienced. For Jesus said, "If I go and prepare a place for you, I will come again, and receive you unto myself; that where I am, there ye may be also" (John 14:3). He has taken leave from a house of God to go to the glorious home of God.

Death can never come unexpectedly for one who is in constant communion with the Saviour. He was prepared for the summons. "Weeping may endure for a night, but joy cometh in the morning" (Psalm 30:5). Death is our servant, not our master. "For all things are yours; whether . . . life, or death" (1 Cor. 3:21-22).

Today because of the shadow that has come to your life, the sun is hidden from you. As children of God, you will remember that when the clouds hang low and your world is dark, the sun still shines; and some day it will break through again. You are comforted in knowing that your loved one has heard the "well done" of the Father, who has said, "Thou hast been faithful over a few things, I will make thee ruler over many things: enter thou into the joy of thy Lord" (Matt. 25:21).

Already he has received his eternal inheritance that Peter mentions: "Blessed be the God and Father of our Lord Jesus Christ, which according to his abundant mercy hath begotten us again unto a lively hope by the resurrection of Jesus Christ from the dead, to an inheritance incorruptible, and undefiled, and that fadeth not away, reserved in heaven for you, who are kept by the power of God through faith unto salvation ready to be revealed in the last time" (1 Peter 1:3-5).

The great revelation has come. The great reunion has begun. In "Friends Beyond," Frederick L. Hosmer has said,

> I cannot think of them as dead,
>   Who walk with me no more;
> Along the path of life I tread—
>   They have but gone before.

This eulogy was delivered at the service of Mrs. Jesse Garrett, who died in an automobile accident. Her husband was pastor of Rosen Heights Baptist Church, Fort Worth, for thirty-three years.

14

The Walk of a Worthy Woman

Proverbs 31:10-31

To us on this earth it often seems that tragedy triumphs—but we know that God always has the last word. All of us recognize that we would not wish Mrs. Garrett to endure the long days and nights of intense suffering that would have been, and we would not question the unknown providence.

As the shock of her death engulfs us in sadness and sorrow, we have to repeat to our own hearts the comforting words of the Lord who has called her, saying: "Thy mission is completed; come up higher." We might aspire to live many days longer, but we could never hope to live half so well.

Purity.—In the last chapter of the book of Proverbs there is the question, "Who can find a virtuous woman? for her price is far above rubies" (v. 10). We are blessed indeed that we can point to such a one. Peter Marshall once said, "We hear about every other kind of women—beautiful women, smart women, sophisticated women, career women, talented women, divorced women, but so seldom do we hear of a godly woman." We have known in Mrs. Garrett that woman.

Nearly sixty-one years ago there was born, the first of three children to a pioneer cattle family in Caldwell, the one you have known affectionately for thirty-three years as Mrs. Jesse Garrett. This marvelous servant of humanity completely submerged her own life in usefulness and lost her life in countless others. The Lord Jesus said, "He that loseth his life for my sake shall find it" (Matt. 10: 39). This was her purpose. Sacrificially she surrendered her life to the needs of those who reached out to her, to those who cried out for her understanding and her compassion. She spent her life in three realms of service. First, she loved with a passion her Lord and his church. Secondly, she was intensely devoted to her family. Then she had a devotion to her community which none of us could equal. We would hasten to say that she was a first citizen in all three realms.

Purpose.—We are here today, not only because we sympathize with her family, but because we acknowledge that a good life pays great dividends. We mourn her passing, and yet we have come to learn from her life. She possessed the secret of how to live a successful life, which is to live it for God. Our Lord said, "Inasmuch as ye have done it unto one of the least of these my brethren, ye have done it unto me" (Matt. 25:40).

A good woman is worthy because "the heart of her husband doth safely trust in her" (Prov. 31:11). Forty-six years ago this woman pledged her heart and her life to Jesse Garrett, now pastor emeritus of this congregation. Blessing after blessing has come to this community and this city because of that union. Fortunate indeed are we that two children, Mary Elizabeth and Jenkins, were born to that marriage. And then six grandchildren came to bless the family as well.

A good woman "will do [her husband] good and not evil all the days of her life," the Bible continues. There are many wonderful pastors' wives, but somehow she was able to excel. Mrs. Garrett did not marry a minister; she married the young man with whom she was in love, a lawyer by profession. But when God called her husband into the ministry, she recognized that she was a part of that calling and she became a good minister's wife. We would crown her today with the laurels of success in that capacity. It could not have been easy to swap a lovely two-story home for a two-room apartment near the Seminary, but she did so without complaint. She was able to learn that which we all must learn—that happiness lies not necessarily in possessions or large houses. Happiness is in the climate of the heart, and home is wherever loving hearts are bound together.

"She . . . worketh willingly with her hands," the Word of God continues. In the book of Acts we find a multitude coming to the bier of a woman named Dorcas and saying, "See what she hath done." If you want to see the monument of Mrs. Garrett, look about you. Remember how she stretched out her hand to you. You are mindful of the flowers that she shared. You remember the food she brought when you were in sickness and in sorrow. We personally remember the touch of her hand on the head of a barefoot boy many years ago. Many girls remember the pat on the cheek by this gentle woman. Many a man here recalls now the encouragement he received from this one whom he greatly respected. Many a woman remembers the inspiration of this one who had lived longer and more wisely and challenged her to a better life.

Praise.—Surely Mrs. Garrett's best epitaph is in the words of her weekly newspaper column, "Cheer Along the Way."

"She stretcheth out her hand to the poor; yea, she reacheth forth her hands to the needy," said the writer in continuing to describe God's ideal woman. There are needs other than physical which claim our hearts, other problems which trouble our souls much more than poverty. When there was discouragement, she was present. When there was spiritual need, she was there. She had a way of putting God in first place in every situation, where he could be seen at all times. She remembered her friends in many ways—frequently with a cheery note. How many hundreds she wrote, not even she could number.

How many times she prayed for you, we cannot say. One told me today, "I was saved because Christ died for me and because Mrs. Garrett prayed for me." Another said, "For seven years the name of a lost person was carried in her glasses case, and each time she opened the case to put on her glasses, it would call her to the remembrance of the name of our lost friend." He is a Christian today and testifies to the power of her prayers.

Surely "Victory Through Prayer" is engraved in the hearts and minds of the people of this congregation, as well as in the prayer room dedicated in her memory. She taught you how to take hold of the power of prayer—one of the primary lessons for Christians to learn. On one hand she taught the children by instruction, on the other hand she taught the adults by example. Even in recent days, she was working with adults in Sunday school and with children in Training Union, holding them together with hands that were affectionately binding.

"She openeth her mouth with wisdom; and in her tongue is the law of kindness" (Prov. 31:26). We think of Mrs. Garrett as a teacher. Hundreds of boys and girls benefitted by her teachings, as under the General Ministers' Association she taught the Bible in our high school. Her tenderness, her example, her truthfulness, her directness, and her humor were all facets of a fully developed and well-packaged personality that pointed her students to Christ.

The words of verses 27 and 28 speak encouragingly to all women: "She looketh well to the ways of her household. . . . Her children arise up, and call her blessed." How Mrs. Garrett could do all this and then raise a family that is a benediction and a blessing, I do not know. But we do know that she never neglected her own, although she sacrificially served others. Her children today rise up and call her blessed. In the words of Solomon: "Her husband also, and he praiseth her."

"A woman that feareth the Lord, she shall be praised" (v. 30). We praise this noble life today because she praised the Lord with her life.

This eulogy was delivered at the service of the Rev. Jesse Garrett, pastor of the Rosen Heights Baptist Church in Fort Worth for thirty-three years, pastor emeritus for seven years.

15

Shepherd of Souls

1 Peter 2:25; 5:4

"Know ye not that there is a prince and a great man fallen this day in Israel?" is a significant question which was asked by a king of his servants in 2 Samuel 3:38. As a servant of the King of kings today, I would answer: yes, a great man of God has laid aside his earthly mantle in exchange for an incorruptible crown. Surely the promise of God in 1 Peter 5:4 is his: "When the chief Shepherd shall appear, ye shall receive a crown of glory that fadeth not away."

A Prince in Israel.—Brother Jesse Garrett, for nearly forty years, has stood tall in this pulpit and in this city. He stood tall before all men because he bowed himself low before God. Our Lord said, "Whosoever shall lose his life for my sake and the gospel's, the same shall save it" (Mark 8:35). This beloved pastor learned early in his ministry the secret of finding through losing. He gave himself completely to God and to the service of his fellowmen.

81

A little mother was coming to the last moments of her life. Her daughter asked her, "Are there any last words?"

The mother replied, "No, I have been saying them all the way."

Brother Garrett has given us his message all along the way. Every day of his life has been an open book to those who have known him. He loved all his people with a great devotion. He was a man happy in his Christian way of life, the only happy existence any man could possibly know. He gave himself completely away to a cause greater than himself and to us all without thought of remuneration or reward.

He was a man of vision, a dreamer of dreams. Forty years ago he was able to see in this rocky hill a Christian Gibraltar. Under the leadership of God, he was able to recognize this as a place to build a great church, a suitable foundation for a living monument to the faith of our fathers.

We might ask, "What are the greatest hours of a great man?" They are not always the public hours; they may be the private hours of a man's devotional life. You treasure yours as I treasure mine. The greatest works of a minister of the gospel probably go unnoticed and unrecognized until the last great day. I remember clearly, however, one of Brother Garrett's inconspicuous hours, a day when he came to a bereaved home to visit. He prayed with a widowed mother and her children and read to them from the family Bible. Before departing, he laid his hand on the head of a boy—my own head—and in so doing, he touched my heart.

Not only did he demonstrate greatness in personal

contacts and greatness in the pulpit, but there was greatness of spirit as well. He asked his people, under the leadership of the Lord, to find someone to succeed him and allow him to retire. When his successor arrived, in the most sincere manner he asked his people to follow their new pastor. He himself became the best follower of all. It takes a great man and a great minister of the gospel to lay aside what men know of "earthly immortality" and to pray for a double portion of the Spirit of God upon his successor as he places his own mantle upon him.

A Giant in the Land.—Brother Garrett was no ordinary man. In the early pages of the "book of beginnings" there appears this statement: "There were giants in the earth in those days" (Gen. 6:4).

This spiritual giant was born about seventy-seven years ago in Burleson County, Texas. His parents were humble people but leaders of their farm community. His father was a physician. It was necessary for Jesse Garrett to leave his home and go to Caldwell to finish high school. By his own efforts he worked his way through law school. After passing his bar examinations, he practiced law for eleven years. Then the call of God's ministry came, and he left his profitable law career and took upon himself the role of a servant of the church of God.

Moving to Fort Worth, he enrolled in Southwestern Baptist Theological Seminary to train for the ministry. It is fitting that today his only son is a trustee of that great school. Through the years, not only did his ministry bless us, but his family as well. His lovely and talented wife, his son Jenkins, his daughter Elizabeth, their companions, and the six wonderful grandchildren—as a family and as a team—have served together in the work of God. A man is a true giant who stands tall before his own family and is able to guide them to his God in reverent and devoted service as this family has been guided to bless this church.

Brother Garrett was a giant in leadership. When he came to serve among us, leadership was not a science but a spirit. There were few rules of church growth or outlined suggestions available. The patterns were cut as the giants, such as this man, moved along! They molded and shaped destinies as only giants can. There were not many large churches forty years ago. Brother Garrett added to the kingdom of God by building one. There were no youth directors and youth programs as such in those days. Being a giant, he saw the problems and challenges of youth and met them by building a youth program.

The financial plan of the church in that day was a continual problem of special offerings—on top of the butter-and-egg and Sunday-by-Sunday gifts. Having a vision thirty years ago, he was able to see the future needs and thus led in the launching of one of the first unified budget programs known.

The memory of this man cannot be confined and imprisoned in a shallow grave. It is engraved in the minds of men and in the hearts of his friends. This church is a monument to Brother Garrett and today we are his beneficiaries. In a college chapel some time ago an educator spoke of another great leader. "If you wish to see this man's monument, look around you." Instinctively, those students in Abilene looked toward the window to see the obvious monument that the man spoken of had built to the glory of God. The sight of this church will continually remind us of Brother Garrett. For he, as other giants who have gone before, has blazed a spiritual path for us to follow.

A Gracious Shepherd.—We are all familiar with the beautiful psalm beginning, "The Lord is my shepherd." How many times Brother Garrett said that to you! And Matthew 9:36 was another reference so often quoted: "They . . . were scattered abroad, as sheep having no shepherd." The great desire of his life was to be a good pastor, a true shepherd of souls, a servant of the Saviour.

He was a princely pastor and a compassionate preacher. He had quick wit and a good sense of humor. He preached to the hearts of men. Lawyer-like and Christlike, he pled for decisions, and that immediately! He believed that the invitation was not simply the climax of the service; rather, it was the service itself. The call to dedication, the call to surrender to Christ was the plea of his words and his heart. He pled with men with the devotion of a father and with the tenderness of a servant. He admonished them, as a prophet, to return to God. He would want this service to remind you that God is the one to be adored, to be praised, to be served. "Surrender to him and all will be well" was Brother Garrett's constant plea. And his aim was, in the words of 1 Peter 2:25, "Ye were as sheep going astray; but are now returned unto the Shepherd and Bishop of your souls."

The Bible reminds us that a good shepherd knows his sheep, and they know his voice. The people of this church followed this shepherd of souls because they believed that he and his wonderful companion, who predeceased him, found their divine marching orders on their knees before God. Knowing God and knowing his people helped to crown this pastor's heart with success. What greater compliment would a Christian want than for it to be said that he spent his life as a servant. For Jesus said, "Whosoever will be great among you . . . shall be servant of all" (Mark 10:43-44).

To his wonderful family, we would say that God has crowned your father with success in every way that a godly man would desire. A minister would want two things more than earthly treasure: to build a great church as his part in the building of the kingdom of God and to raise his family to revere God. We believe that Brother Garrett has been rewarded in both these efforts.

To those who followed this shepherd through all these years we would say, "Follow on!" For the shepherd has but gone up higher to be with his Master—the Great Shepherd. We know that there have not been many really happy days since that fateful day in June some years ago when his companion went away. We do know that there has been a great effort on the part of this people to make these sunset years the best years of his life. God has rewarded him, for "the best is yet to be."

I am sure he would say, in the words of the apostle Paul, "Therefore, my beloved brethren, be ye stedfast, unmoveable, always abounding in the work of the Lord, forasmuch as ye know that your labour is not in vain in the Lord" (1 Cor. 15:58). We can say with Job, "The Lord gave, and the Lord hath taken away; blessed be the name of the Lord" (1:21).

All of us know that the song "Blest Be the Tie" was Brother Garrett's doxology, his testimony, his joy. In the great hours of this church he would have the people sing together, "Blest be the tie that binds our hearts in Christian love." When he went home to be with God it was his greatest hour. Those who loved him best will rejoice with him. Therefore, let us sing this song together as our benediction and as a fitting tribute to the climax of his noble life.

16

Calling Children

Suggested Bible Verses for an Infant

"He shall feed his flock like a shepherd: he shall gather the lambs with his arm, and carry them in his bosom" (Isa. 40:11).

"Jesus . . . said unto them, Suffer the little children to come unto me, and forbid them not: for of such is the kingdom of God. Verily I say unto you, Whosoever shall not receive the kingdom of God as a little child, he shall not enter therein. And he took them up in his arms, put his hands upon them, and blessed them" (Mark 10: 14-16).

"David therefore besought God for the child; and David fasted, and went in, and lay all night upon the earth. . . . And it came to pass on the seventh day, that the child died. And the servants of David feared to tell him that the child was dead. . . . But when David saw that his servants whispered, David perceived that the child was dead: therefore David said unto his servants, Is the child dead? And they said, He is dead.

"Then David arose from the earth, and washed, and anointed himself, and changed his apparel, and came into the house of the Lord, and worshipped: then he came to his own house; and when he required, they set bread before him, and he did eat.

"Then said his servants unto him, What thing is this that thou hast done? thou didst fast and weep for the child, while it was alive; but when the child was dead, thou didst rise and eat bread. And he said, While the child was yet alive, I fasted and wept: for I said, Who can tell whether God will be gracious to me, that the child may live? But now he is dead, wherefore should I fast? can I bring him back again? I shall go to him, but he shall not return to me" (2 Sam. 12:16-23).

Hannah, the mother of Samuel said, "For this child I prayed; and the Lord hath given me my petition which I asked of him: therefore also I have lent him to the Lord" (1 Sam. 1:27-28).

"Is it well with the child? And she answered, It is well" (2 Kings 4:26).

"The Lord gave, and the Lord hath taken away; blessed be the name of the Lord" (Job 1:21).

"I say unto you, That in heaven their angels do always behold the face of my Father which is in heaven" (Matt. 18:10).

"They shall be mine, saith the Lord of hosts, in that day when I make up my jewels" (Mal. 3:17).

"Jesus said, Suffer little children, and forbid them not,

to come unto me: for of such is the kingdom of heaven" (Matt. 19:14).

"It is not the will of your Father which is in heaven, that one of these little ones should perish" (Matt. 18:14).

"The eternal God is thy refuge, and underneath are the everlasting arms" (Deut. 33:27).

Prayer.—Our Father, we know that thou dost understand our hearts, for thou hast said, "Like as a father pitieth his children, so the Lord pitieth them that fear him." The aching hearts of these parents, O God, thou dost know, for thy Word hath said, "As one whom his mother comforteth, so will I comfort you." We know that thou art mindful of their loss, even as we are mindful that thou didst give thy only begotten Son to us.

Thou hast numbered the sands of the sea. Thou dost see the sparrows that fall. Thou dost number daily the hairs of our heads. O Lord, the tears of these loved ones do not go unnoticed in thy sight. And in that perfect day, thou wilt wipe away all tears from our eyes. We thank thee that thou art here with us and that thou hast never forsaken us. Amen.

Calling a Child

"The disciples [came] unto Jesus, saying, Who is the greatest in the kingdom of heaven? And Jesus called a little child unto him, and set him in the midst of them" (Matt. 18:1-2).

Death is sad at any age, but our feelings concerning death are not always of the same degree. It is most difficult for us to associate the cradle with the coffin because one represents the beginning and the other the end of life. It is always sad to see a star glimmer for a little while and then fade away. We are always saddened when the symphony of life is cut short. God would remind us that this "bud which gave promise of the fairest bloom" has not faded but has rather been transplanted into the eternal garden of God.

Our God, who is the Father of all, understands the parents' heartache. Did he not say, "Like as a father pitieth his children, so the Lord pitieth them that fear him" (Psalm 103:13)? He would comfort our hearts, for he said, "As one whom his mother comforteth, so will I comfort you" (Isa. 66:13).

Our blessed Lord has always heard the Rachels weeping for their children. The "cry of Ramah" has come down to us. The tears of Hagar have not ceased to flow. The sob of David for Absalom is continually felt. But our sympathetic Saviour still asks, "Why weepest thou?"

Certainty.—It is a certainty that our Father knows far better than we ourselves concerning the needs of little children. We have the certainty that Jesus loved little children and that he has identified himself with them: "Whoso shall receive one such little child in my name receiveth me" (Matt. 18:5). He reached out for them and touched them and blessed them. He warned against any who would offend these little ones. We have the certainty that he came to save little children, for he said, "Except ye be converted, and become as little children, ye shall not enter into the kingdom of heaven" (Matt. 18:3).

We have the certainty that he understands little children, for does he not know all things, and was he not born as a babe, and did he not grow as a child? We have the certainty that he provides a better place for them—far better than even the marvelous imaginations of wondering children can dream. How blessed are we in having a faith that makes so large a place for the children!

Contentment.—When the gifted poet, Edgar Guest, lost his little daughter, he composed the poem, "If They Could Write."

> What glorious news they'd have to tell
> If only they could write today,
> Those who have gone afar to dwell
> Where all the glorious spirits stay.
>
> In fancy then I set it down,
> What Marjorie would pen for me—
> "I've touched the hem of Jesus' gown
> The way they did in Galilee."
>
> And thinking thus, I am content
> To bear the loneliness and wait,
> Because I know her days are spent
> In all the company of the great.

The only possible contentment that a parent can find is in the realization that the child is eternally safe. They will never know any further hurt; they will escape the sorrow that this world brings. The little children who slip away to heaven early in life are especially blessed. "To die is gain" at any age.

Children know this Christlike contentment, for Jesus said, "Yea; have ye never read, Out of the mouth of babes . . . thou hast perfected praise?" (Matt. 21:16). This was true in the statement of a little child who had just heard of the death of a playmate: "She is luckier than we are. She got to go to heaven first."

Comfort.—In ancient days Jacob mourned for his son Joseph whom he thought was dead. Joseph was not dead but was alive and living in another country. Does it not comfort our hearts today to know that this little one is more alive than ever before? She is living in her heavenly home, which the writer of the book of Hebrews has called "a better country" (11:16).

Shakespeare has said, "Everyone can master grief, but he who has it." Our only mastery comes in our recognition of the presence of Christ and in the knowledge that he cares. "For we have not an high priest which cannot be touched with the feeling of our infirmities" (Heb. 4:15). We are comforted with David that even though the child cannot return to us, we may go to him. Even now our hearts turn homeward, as we think of Long-fellow's "Resignation."

> She is not dead,—the child of our affection,
>   But gone unto that school
> Where she no longer needs our poor protection,
>   And Christ himself doth rule.

Acknowledgments

Chapter 3—Rand McNally & Company, Hammond, Indiana, for permission to use the poem "Faith," by Ella Wheeler Wilcox.

Chapter 7—Harper & Row, Publishers, Incorporated, New York City, for permission to use the quotation from "The Memory of the Just," by Clarence Macartney included in *The Funeral Encyclopedia*, edited by Charles L. Wallis.

Chapter 8—Doubleday & Company, Incorporated, New York City, for permission to reprint "When Earth's Last Picture Is Painted," by Rudyard Kipling.

Chapter 9—Juanita J. Miller, Oakland, California, for permission to use the poem "The Greatest Battle," by Joaquin Miller. Fleming H. Revell Company, Westwood, New Jersey, for the use of the quotation by Sydney Smith from *I Quote*, by Virginia Ely.

Chapter 10—Fleming H. Revell Company, Westwood, New Jersey, for the use of the quotation by D. L. Moody.

Chapter 13—Harper & Row, Publishers, Incorporated, New York City, for permission to reprint the poems "Well Done," by James Montgomery, and "Friends Beyond," by Frederick L. Hosmer, from *Masterpieces of Religious Verse*, edited by James D. Morrison.

Chapter 14—Fleming H. Revell Company, Westwood, New Jersey, for permission to use the quotation from *Mr. Jones, Meet the Master*, by Peter Marshall.

Chapter 16—Harper & Row, Publishers, Incorporated, New York City, for permission to reprint the poem "Resignation," by Henry W. Longfellow, from *Masterpieces of Religious Verse*, edited by James D. Morrison. Reilly & Lee Company, Chicago, for permission to use the poem "If They Could Write," by Edgar Guest.

Bibliography

ALLEN, CHARLES L. *When You Lose a Loved One.* Westwood, N. J.: Fleming H. Revell Co., 1959.

BARTON, F. M. (ed.). *One Thousand Thoughts for Funeral Occasions.* New York: Harper and Bros., 1912.

BLACKWOOD, ANDREW WATTERSON. *The Funeral.* Philadelphia: Westminster Press, 1942.

BONNER, WILLIAM JONES. *When Sorrow Comes.* Anderson, Ind.: Warner Press, 1958.

CHILES, JOHN R. *A Treasury of Funeral Messages.* Grand Rapids: Baker Book House, 1960.

CHRISTENSEN, JAMES L. *The Minister's Service Handbook.* Westwood, N. J.: Fleming H. Revell Co., 1960.

COHEN, O. R. *The Light Shines Through.* Boston: Little, Brown, & Co., 1928.

DONIGER, SIMON (ed.). *Bereavement—Death—The Funeral.* Great Neck, N. Y.: Pastoral Psychology Press, 1955.

FORD, W. HERSCHEL. *Simple Sermons for Funeral Services.* Grand Rapids: Zondervan Publishing House, 1962.

GOLLADAY, R. E. *The Light in the Window.* Grand Rapids: Zondervan Publishing House, 1937.

GOODRICH, ROBERT E., JR. *On the Other Side of Sorrow.* New York: Abingdon Press, 1962.

GRAHAM, ROSCOE. *Remembered with Love.* New York: American Press, 1961.

HALLOCK, G. B. F. (ed.). *Cyclopedia of Funeral Sermons and Sketches.* New York: George H. Doran Co., 1926.

HOBBS, J. R. *The Pastor's Manual.* Nashville: Broadman Press, 1933.

IRION, PAUL E. "The Funeral, an Experience of Value." An Address Given at the Convention of the National Funeral Directors Association, at Milwaukee, Wisconsin, October 24, 1956.

————. *Funeral and the Mourners*. Nashville: Abingdon Press, 1954.

KETCHAM, WILLIAM E. (ed.). *Funeral Sermons and Outline Addresses*. New York: Harper and Bros., 1899.

LEACH, WILLIAM HERMAN (ed.). *The Improved Funeral Manual*. Grand Rapids: Baker Book House, 1956.

LEE, ROBERT G. *For the Time of Tears*. Grand Rapids: Zondervan Publishing House, 1950.

MACMILLAN, HUGH, *et. al. The Divine Artist*. Manchester: James Robinson, 1903.

MEYER, F. B. *Peace, Perfect Peace*. Westwood, N. J.: Fleming H. Revell, Co., 1909.

————, *et. al. Funeral Sermons and Outlines*. Grand Rapids: Baker Book House, 1951.

Sowing in Tears, Reaping in Joy. Burlington, Iowa: German Literary Board, 1912.

VAN WYK, WILLIAM P. *My Notes for Addresses at Funeral Occasions*. Grand Rapids: Baker Book House, 1955.

WALLACE, ARCHER. *In Grateful Remembrance*. New York: Abingdon Press, 1955.

WALLIS, CHARLES L. (ed.). *The Funeral Encyclopedia*. New York: Harper and Bros., 1953.

WHEELER, E. J. (ed.). *Pulpit and Grave*. New York: Funk & Wagnalls Co., 1884.

YOUNG, RICHARD K. *The Pastor's Hospital Ministry*. Nashville: Broadman Press, 1954.